WHISPERS OF MY HEART!

VERSES OF LOVE AND FEELINGS

JOJO D'SOUZA

This book is dedicated to:

My mother, Lorna

Her unwavering love, encouragement, and the countless hours she spent nurturing my reading and writing skills have been the foundation of my creative journey.

Mum, your spirit continues to inspire every word I write.

My wife, Rajkumari

You are the love of my life, the heart of our home, and the glue that binds our family together. Your steadfast support and endless love make everything possible.

My children, Ankita and Taran

You are my greatest blessing and the reason I strive to capture the beauty and complexity of life in my words.

I see a reflection of us in both of you.

My sister, Louella, my cousins, our families and friends

For always being there for me, sharing in the laughter, and standing by me through every storm. Your love and support have been a constant source of strength throughout my life.

With all my heart, I thank you all.

Contents

Foreword

I am thrilled to present my dear friend Jojo's debut
poetry collection, "Whispers of My Heart."
Having always enjoyed Jojo's spontaneous writing, I am happy
that he has finally decided to share his creativity with the world.
His ability to capture and celebrate the essence of feelings in his
poems is truly remarkable. Jojo, your words have the power to
touch hearts and inspire minds.
As you embark on this incredible journey, I wish you all the
success and joy that you so richly deserve.
All the best, always.

Deepak Anant Bandekar
Founder,
Big Banner Entertainment and Media LLP

Preface

For as long as I can remember, writing verse, rhyme, and poetry has been my way of capturing the essence of moments, emotions, and relationships. My words have often found their home in the hearts of family and friends, serving as personal tributes to those I hold dear. Crossing the golden age of fifty brought a profound shift in my perspective. A major health issue became a poignant reminder of life's fragility, followed closely by the irreplaceable loss of my beloved mum.

These experiences also underscored the importance of cherishing every moment and expressing our innermost thoughts and feelings.

While my storytelling has often taken the form of films, crafted from tales I have woven, it became clear that the time had come to share my poetry with a wider audience. "Whispers of My Heart" is the culmination of this realisation - an intimate reflection of my life, capturing the joys, sorrows, and myriad moods that define our existence. It is my hope that these poems resonate with you, offering a glimpse into the love, pain, and beauty that have coloured my world. As you turn each page, may you find solace, inspiration, and a connection to the whispers of my heart.

Acknowledgements

Ina Peres da Silva
Deepak, Chandan and Aryan Bandekar
Deepa Anant Bandekar
Dr. Cidalia Bodade
Mr. Umesh Sinha

*****

Your presence in my life has been a source of immense inspiration and support. Thank you for being part of my journey and for the profound impact you'll have on my life.

"In every word I write and blend,
Your love and support, I truly commend.
Thank you for believing, right from the start,
You've penned your place within my heart."

Prologue

In the quiet moments of reflection, when life's symphony played both its most harmonious and dissonant chords, I found solace in words. "Whispers of My Heart" is more than a collection of poems; it is the essence of my journey, captured through time.

Each verse here is a fragment of my soul, carefully penned during moments of joy, sorrow, love, and contemplation. These words are born from my personal experiences, some of which were shaped by a brush with mortality that irrevocably altered my outlook on life. This near-death experience acted as a catalyst, transforming my perspective and infusing each line with newfound depth and meaning.

This book is a testament to the power of resilience and the enduring human spirit. It is an offering to anyone who seeks to find comfort, inspiration, or a companion in their own journey. The wishes and greetings interwoven within these pages are meant to be shared, customised, and adapted, so they may resonate with your own experiences and emotions.

May you find as much peace and inspiration in these words as I found in writing them.

1. To Mum, with love!

I had to start my first chapter with a tribute to the woman who made me who I am today. My mother, Lorna D'Souza. I penned this a week after she passed, as I was still coming to terms with the fact that she wasn't going to be around anymore.

REFLECTIONS

In reflections, I glimpse your smile,

In shadows, as I rest a while.

Time dances swiftly, fleeting by,

Yet memories of you will never die.

From childhood's innocence, you guided me,

Moulded the person I came to be.

Why did you leave, so swiftly depart?

I thought we'd more moments to impart.

No longer do you pass my bedroom door,

Yet in my thoughts, you linger more.

Each day we miss you, your love was so fine,

But in my heart, your presence does shine.

Oh, mother dear, so gentle, so kind,

In your absence, solace I seek to find.

Though you've journeyed beyond the shore,

Your love lives on.. forevermore.

A Heavenly Birthday Wish

In the gentle breeze, your whispers I hear,
Mom, your love forever near.
Though parted by time, our bond still strong,
In memories sweet, you'll forever belong.
On this day, your spirit shines bright,
A beacon of love, a guiding light.
Ninety years of grace, strength and love,
Your legacy soars on wings above.
An angel now, in heaven above,
Watching over us with endless love.
In every star that twinkles at night,
I feel your presence, a guiding light.
Mom, my hero, forever adored,
In my heart, you'll never be ignored.
Happy birthday, in realms unseen,
Your love endures, eternal, serene.

A Tribute From A Granddaughter To Her Grandma

In memory's embrace, a cherished light,
Granny, a beacon, ever bright.
Teacher's wisdom, captain's pride,
In your presence, hearts abide.
Graceful in every step you took,
Beauty echoed in every look.
Kindness flowed in every word,
In your embrace, love was stirred.
A life of lessons, gently taught,
In every mind, your legacy wrought.
With patience, you shaped the young,
In every soul, your song was sung.
Beside the captain, your heart did sail,
Through every storm, love did prevail.
A bond unbroken, firm and true,
In every voyage, shared with you.
Loved by all who felt your grace,
In every heart, you found a place.
Granny dear, forever in our sight,
A guiding star, through day and night.

Fare Thee Well, Mum!

In a better place, a happier space you dwell
Your legacy of joy, love, and grace we will tell.
United finally with your husband Joe, so dear
Celebrating a past that's now crystal clear.
The emptiness, a poignant echo, so profound
The silence in our house where love was abound.
Rest in peace, these words we gently pray
Forever missed, in our hearts you'll stay.
Each night, each day, we feel your absence keen
In memories cherished, your presence still seen.
Though separated by a vast divide
Love's bond with you will forever abide.
Rest now, dear mother, in eternal peace
Your love and light will never cease.
In our hearts, you'll always stay
Guiding us along life's winding way.

A Birthday Wish for Deepa Tai
- A dear Family Friend

For everything that you've been..
A mother, a mentor, a friend, a guide
Amazing as always, our joy, our pride
With each year that passes
You grow younger with grace
We've grown with the love of your warm embrace
May each day be happy and blessed from above
Happy birthday from all of us with lots of love..

2. Feelings!

Death Is The Most Beautiful Sleep

Death is the most beautiful sleep.
A bliss filled peace, whilst others weep.
No one knows yet, what lies yonder,
Heaven, Hell or reincarnation, I wonder...
Death, is the most beautiful sleep.
No care, no fear, just emptiness so deep
Death is the only predictable future known
Everyone dies there's nothing we own..
Some call death, when this life they can't handle
Some fade out like a long burning candle
Some age and die, peaceful at last
Death is the most beautiful sleep
And yet there's a shadow cast
Death is the most beautiful sleep
Slow, long, early or fast...

JOJO D'SOUZA

A Shadow Of Doubt

Happy exteriors...Broken interiors

What is it he feared the most?

A heart that's crumbling,

like burnt morning toast.

A Shadow of doubt,

runs constantly, throughout

Her actions speak,

of secret liaisons they wreak.

The blame, an excuse. When he leaves, they connect.

Happy exteriors, Broken interiors,

nothing else disturbs him more..

He wants to fly, to be without doubt

But can she be trusted, when he steps out?

The past he's buried, but she's blind to that change

New experiences, she finds, they add colour to her range.

Happy exteriors- Broken interiors

How long must he keep trying?

While deep inside, he's frying...

with hurt and pain and sometimes rage

His one solid rock has found another exciting stage

Behind closed doors, without

a shadow of doubt.

Don't Hide Behind A Happy Smile

What lies behind that happy smile
Would you climb over My minds hidden stile?
Questions aflutter, like birds in a cage
Filling me up, like a pressure cooker in rage
What lies beyond, Those bright happy eyes,
A fake sense of belonging, in a broken world of lies?
Don't judge me, when you know not what I feel
My heart bleeds tears, that rust my nerves of steel.
Life is a game, that saying is old,
You need balls of brass today, Not a heart of gold
Reach out they say, talk to people who care
But when that time does come, Is anyone really there?
What lies beyond that happy smile?
What's hidden in my lonely soul?
What hurts so much I'd rather die?
The answer is our biggest lie -
We say we're fine, When we are not,
We hide alone, So deep in thought.
We process until, We Overheat,
And then go on - Repeat, repeat
Don't hide behind a happy smile.
Find ways to shed your pain.
I do it best by writing verse,
Or crying in the rain.

A New Year Wish

For the friendship
that you've given me
For the special things
you've done,
This comes to hope our
NEW YEAR
Will be a very special one.
For the good times and
the bad ones
For times we laughed
or cried,
We held our hands
and walked together,
Always side by side.
With you I wish that each day
Will always inspire a rhyme
I pray our love will bind us
Every single time.
HAPPY NEW YEAR!

Once Bitten, Twice Shy

I'll never break your trust again...
I broke it once, I felt the pain.
Once bitten twice shy,
It's so often said
Trust when it's broken
Makes you - inside - feel dead
Realising from within
That's really the key
Coming clear and clean
Is what sets you free
I'll never break your trust again,
I'll never let you feel that pain
Together, our lives we'll once more regain
With love and laughter and dances in the rain.

3. Love! Love! Love!

You Glisten like Raindrops...

You glisten

like raindrops

on green leaves,

Like oil

on fresh raw skin,

I listen to the sound

of your laughter,

Happiness I feel

within.

I'm not weak

without you,

But you definitely make me

Stronger

I have you safe

in my arms each day

To love you so much

Longer....

Flow...

Thoughts flow,
Like your hair
across your face
I love when we are in,
our cozy happy space
I know words don't
always sustain
The way I feel,
Like the unpredictable rain
Sweating it out at yoga,
A full body glow
Style defines you,
In anything you wear
Your beauty is always
in full flow.
I feel you,
I understand too
Life doesn't mean
anything,
Without you being
In everything
that I do.

Countless Memories – A Treasure Trove

Near death,
a glimpse of what may be,
But in that moment,
we truly see.
Living oblivious,
Death's gentle touch,
Teaching us life,
we cherish so much.
With countless memories,
a treasure trove,
And newfound hope,
we bravely rove.
Crafting a path,
with blessings to guide,
With love as our compass,
we'll joyously stride.
I write every moment
and this just came to me
I'm sure together
we'll create
a masterpiece to see.

A Comforting Wish...

In grace she walks,
a humble sight,
Radiant with kindness,
pure and bright.
With respect
and compassion,
her heart does shine,
In every gesture,
a woman divine.
Yet burdened she feels,
by some extra weight's toll,
Shadows of the past
darken her beautiful soul.
Trusting and loving,
perhaps too soon,
Leaves her heart vulnerable,
Like a filled up balloon
Cooking, a task, she'd rather evade,
In pots and pans, her patience does fade.
But above everything else,
her beauty still gleams,
She'll fight to succeed
To achieve her dreams.

Love has a Thousand Meanings

"*Love has a thousand meanings and yet is only an empty four letter word if there is no feeling attached. Young love is passionate and as we grow older and wiser it opens up to mean trust above all. Knowing someone so well, for so long can take it's toll and that's where love should be binding, like glue.*

Love needs a recharge or a top-up and that's where many people drift apart - They don't recharge.

Through ups and downs in the journey of life, it is always important to rekindle the spark to keep the flame of your love burning and that in turn will keep your relationship alive."

Love is friendship, Love is trust, Love is remembering that we're all born from dust. Love is being patient, love is being kind, love means the woman's always right, gentlemen, please don't mind."

4. Family Time!

To My Beloved wife, Rajkumari ~~~

Taurus like my mother,
steadfast and true,
Solid as a rock,
in all that you do.
My anchor in life's tempest,
you keep me grounded,
Your efficiency and grace
leave all astounded.
Beautiful as a rose, in fresh bloom,
Turning heads always, whenever you enter a room.
Creative, talented, and full of life,
You keep me beaming, my wonderful wife.
Your expressions speak louder
than words can scream,
To you, my beloved,
let's live out our dream.

To My Daughter Ankita, With Love ~~~

My beautiful honey-bunny,
the world is your stage
Spread your wings in the limelight,
As you write a new page.
Touch the sky with grace, as your spirit soars,
Feel our warm embrace, love endlessly pours.
You're a woman of intellectual grace,
I'll always hold your hand,
in this enchanting space.
Lead you beyond the stars,
where dreams align,
An artist , a director, a daughter divine.
You're my shining star, in the cosmic art,
In every scene, you play your part.
Together we'll weave tales,
of stars and light,
In the theater of life,
let your story take flight...
To everyone you meet, all over the world,
May each step bring delight
As you travel the world and
Keep shining bright.

A Symphony for my son Taran ~~~

In Taran and Ankita,
we see the best of us both,
Each of you unique,
keeping us afloat.
A musician with talent,
Taran, you make us proud,
Luckily, we've sailed through
without neighbours shouting out,
"It's too damn loud."
You play many instruments,
and design sound that's blazing,
Quiet and brilliant,
people find your
curls amazing.
Like the music you compose,
may your life be
balanced too,
Here's wishing you
all the best
as you rock life's
symphonies through.

To My Sister Louella ~~~

God blessed me with one sister,
He gave me you.
Together we sailed through
storms and fires, we stuck together
like glue.
Through ups and downs,
we've always been connected,
Your strong will and talent
often reflected.
In the things you do,
you take great pride,
As an older brother,
I'll always be by your side.

5. Wishes & Greetings!

A Birthday Wish for a friend to his Wife .

In a world where dreams unfold,
A wonderful soul, a go-getter bold.
You accomplish anything in your targeted view,
With your heart of gold, That's pure and true.
Warm and kind, misunderstood at times,
Yet, you shine bright, Like radiant rhymes.
A star to many, a guiding light,
On your birthday, wishes and blessings
with love, take flight.
May your day be special and bright,
With joy and laughter, pure delight.
My best to you, always in sight,
A beacon of love,
through the darkest night.

Happy Birthday Reshu

To Reshu, our dynamic spark,
may your birthday be bright,
A doll with a temper,
yet your heart's always right.
You talk at a fast pace
that leaves us in awe,
An adventurous spirit,
who follows no law.
Pageants and motherhood,
You've conquered with flair,
But your care and your kindness
are beyond compare.
On this special day,
may your dreams all come true,
Happy Birthday, dear Reshu,
three cheers from us too!

"Birthday's are always special. Recalling some random
birthday wishes sent to family and friends .."

Happy Birthday Divya

Dr. Divya Rani, our shining star,
A doctor, a queen, a dream afar.
With a heart so kind and
a mind so bright,
You can get people unconscious
without a fight
On this special day,
we celebrate you,
For all the amazing things
we've been through..
A dreamer, a healer,
a true inspiration,
You bring us joy and
complete admiration.
Happy birthday, Divya,
with love so grand,
May your year be magical,
perfectly unplanned.
In every smile and
every cheer,
Know that you're cherished,
know that you're dear.

Happy Birthday Anila

On your birthday, dear Gullu,
May peace and health
be showered upon you.
Your straightforward style
is a strength indeed,
Though toes you may step on,
you're always there in times of need.
With a bubbling spirit
and a heart that's true,
May your special day be
as amazing as you!
Here's wishing you a birthday
that's Happy all year through
and an extra wish to say
get well too.

"In the good old days of writing by hand or using a typewriter, creativity was fluent and flowing from the heart to paper. Today in an AI world, my note to all aspiring writers is that AI may replace your words but it can never replace your soul or your spirit."

Happy Birthday Marylou

On your special day,
let's shout and holler,
You're one in a million,
standing taller.
A friend, a cousin,
and a lawyer too,
With a heart of gold,
shining through.
Your piano skills, par excellence,
Bring joy to all those around.
A mischievous soul, with laughter
that shakes the ground.
You're a fabulous mother
a reliable friend.
Here's to another year, younger,
And a bond that will last till the end
Happy birthday to you, dear Mary Lou,
May joy and love surround you,
with loads of happiness too.

Happy Birthday Amira

Happy birthday, dear Amira,
my partner in crime,
We've shared many moments,
through laughter and time.
Remember the day
that we short-circuited
your house?
An experiment gone wild,
our secret, our rouse.
We've faced heart issues, both you and I,
But together we're soaring, let's
reach for the sky.
Recovering strong, with love as our guide,
With family by our side, it's been
a fantastic ride...
So here's to you, Amira,
on your special day,
May joy and health
in your life always stay.
Let's cherish each moment, powered by love,
And blessings from our parents,
sent from above.

Happy Birthday Aryan

On this special day, let's cheer and sing,
For Aryan's now turned sweet sixteen!
A heart full of wanderlust, eager to explore,
From bustling cities to the sunny seashore.
A lover of cars, with engines that roar,
Driving through life, always craving much more.
Art and craft, a creative flair,
With every thing you do,
you show how much you care.
A foodie at heart, loving every bite,
Good times with friends
brings pure delight.
With a love for humanity, so deep and true,
Your kindness and wisdom, always shine through.
Happy Birthday, Aryan! Here's to you,
May your travels be thrilling
and skies always blue.
May your art be inspired
and your days be full of cheer,
Wishing you joy and
an amazing year!

~ *HAPPY ANNIVERSARY* ~

May your path be blessed
with strength and grace,
In every step, may you both
find your place.
Through the highs and lows,
together you'll stand,
Hand in hand, heart in heart,
across the land.
May the love you share
grow ever bright,
Guiding your steps
in the darkest night.
Together, may your journey be long,
In laughter and love,
forever strong.
Happy anniversary,
with wishes so true,
May blessings, love and strength
always be with you.

6. Bits and Wits!

She Kissed Me.

She kissed me in the morning,
She kissed me in the night.
She kissed me when I entered,
She kissed me left and right
She kissed me when I drove her
She kissed me when I parked
She kissed me when I fed her and then
wagged her tail and barked.

* * *

"An ode to all the beautiful animals I've had. Remembering Suzie, Lassie and Lucky. Suzie was an African Grey parrot that was with us for a long long time. She was often walking or moving about freely and could say a few words as well. "Water, my darling" was a sentence my mum would say to her whenever she filled her water bowl, a sentence that Suzie was reknowned for saying.

Humour has been the one thing that has kept me going and the ability to see the funny side of everything, has kept my engine running... I think I'm funny. I really do!"

I think I'm Funny!

I think I'm funny,
hilarious at times,
I laugh at my own jokes,
no need for signs.
Most of the time,
I'm cracking up free,
Others join in,
as jolly as can be.
But then there are those,
who sigh in pure grief,
Begging for silence,
praying for relief.
Some stare at me,
their jaws open wide,
Seeking heavenly escape
from my comedic tide.

A Bike Ride in the Rain

We're out on a bike ride, it's quite a thrill,
With my wife in control,I take the pillion still.
She's one in a billion,
that's clear to see.
With her, riding through the rain,
our spirits roaming free.
Droplets fall like tender kisses,
But with the wind,
it feels like bullet-misses.
Through bumpy roads, I bounce and sway,
A new adventure, come what may.
A bike ride through the city's maze,
New moments that forever amaze.
Just being with her, makes me proud,
My heart races, my love unbowed.
We zigzag through
the bustling town,
My Radiant Princess,
with her invisible crown.

Writing A Rhyme

More than poetry, Ive always prided myself on my ability to rhyme. Or at least come close to a word or a phrase that can be rhymed. The toughest I was ever asked was at a conference. A Reporter looked at me dead-straight in the eye and said "Rhyme Orange". Flummoxed for a few seconds, and being the nerdy-quick-wit that I was back in the day, I replied. "A Rhymer who can't rhyme orange, shows he has no-range, Isn't that a shame when you have no game, now do you want me to rhyme duck?" The trick I use is to repeat the word thinking of all the alphbets that I can and randomly start muttering them in my mind. This helps. Some words like year, dear, near, fear are simple and catchy. You, due, new, few. The Second trick is to find an easy word to rhyme as you end the sentence so that you can match your end words with a corresponding rhyme. **Example: "Here's wishing you a birthday, filled with cake and cream. Blessed with good health, go fulfil your biggest dream".** A rhyme a day keeps your mind active. Husband and purple are difficult to rhyme, believe me I've tried it, many a time. So are purple and orange and month, and here I'm being completely blunt. Happy Rhyming

- Jojo (jojodsouzagoa@gmail.com)

Quotes & Verses

- *The future belongs to those who believe in the POWER of their Dreams.*
- *The best way to make your dreams come true is to wake up and get to work.*
- *Cheers to the years gone by and ahead!*
- *A lesson from my Mum: "If you can't emote, write it in rhyme, it will always work, every single time."*
- *Never mess with a writer or a film maker. We could turn you into a nightmare in our next book or make you the comic misfit in a movie, or even kill you happily. (lol)*
- *Love comes, love goes, trust is the most important binding factor in a relationship with anyone.*
- *Don't say. **"DO!"** Actions always speak louder than words.*
- *A woman is not the weaker sex. She's the sex that makes you weaker.*
- *Don't judge others. Seeing is not believing. Believe me when I say all your senses can decieve you. Think before you "react".*
- *The greatest film ever made is LIFE!*

❧❧❧

And that brings us to the end of the first Volume of Whispers of my Heart.

Should I end with a rhyme or maybe a verse? A poem or a word or two, I could write something especially for you.

Please let me know, what you desire, I could write to please or set a heart on fire.

• 34 •

Thank you all for being a part of my journey. My heart will keep whispering and the writing will continue to flow...